Picture Perfect

Small Stitcheries and Embroidered Niceties

Kathy Schmitz

Martingale®
Create with Confidence

Picture Perfect: Small Stitcheries and Embroidered Niceties
© 2019 by Kathy Schmitz

Martingale®
19021 120th Ave. NE, Ste. 102
Bothell, WA 98011-9511 USA
ShopMartingale.com

Printed in China
24 23 22 21 20 19   8 7 6 5 4 3 2 1

Library of Congress Cataloging-in-Publication Data

Names: Schmitz, Kathy, author.

Title: Picture perfect : small stitcheries and embroidered niceties / Kathy Schmitz.

Description: Bothell, WA : Martingale, [2019] | Summary: "The 16 little sewing and embroidery designs in this book were created to stitch up quickly and easily for immediate results! Also included are several examples of ways these tiny stitcheries can be used"-- Provided by publisher.

Identifiers: LCCN 2019026060 | ISBN 9781683560401 (paperback)

Subjects: LCSH: Embroidery--Patterns. | Decoration and ornament.

Classification: LCC TT771 .S36 2019 | DDC 746.44041--dc23

LC record available at https://lccn.loc.gov/2019026060

MISSION STATEMENT

We empower makers who use fabric and yarn
to make life more enjoyable.

CREDITS

**PUBLISHER AND
CHIEF VISIONARY OFFICER**
Jennifer Erbe Keltner

CONTENT DIRECTOR
Karen Costello Soltys

DESIGN MANAGER
Adrienne Smitke

MANAGING EDITOR
Tina Cook

PRODUCTION MANAGER
Regina Girard

**ACQUISITIONS AND
DEVELOPMENT EDITOR**
Laurie Baker

**COVER AND
BOOK DESIGNER**
Kathy Kotomaimoce

TECHNICAL EDITOR
Ellen Pahl

LOCATION PHOTOGRAPHER
Adam Albright

COPY EDITOR
Durby Peterson

STUDIO PHOTOGRAPHER
Brent Kane

ILLUSTRATOR
Sandy Loi

SPECIAL THANKS
*Photography for this book was taken at
the home of Julie Smiley in Des Moines, Iowa.*

Contents

5
Introduction

7
Redwork Houses

15
Bluework Birds

23
Pretty Pillows

31
Garden Decor

39
Bowl Fillers
and Sachets

49
Note Cards

54
Embroidery Basics

60
Decorative Mats
for Framing

79
Embroidery
Pattern Index

79
Resources

80
About the Author

bird

Introduction

For me, being in the middle of a huge embroidery project is kind of like being in the middle of a really good book. I look forward to working on it, and I love that I can pick it up and continue whenever I want.

The majority of the time, however, I crave instant gratification. The 16 little designs in this book are quick to stitch for immediate results! And they're all the same size so you can mix and match them to frame as unique artwork for your walls or make a sachet to give as a hostess gift. You can also make a special note card for your best friend or a sweet pillow for your home.

My favorite part of this book is the selection of watercolor mats you'll find at the back (see page 60). These are meant to be cut out or photocopied and used behind your framed embroidered pieces as I've done. There are three different designs, and I've provided three copies of each design—perfect if you want to stitch an entire grouping to frame and display together. Or, if you want to stitch only one or two, each watercolor mat has a garden-themed quotation in the center, so you can frame and enjoy the artwork as is.

These mats are my original watercolor designs, and I hope you'll enjoy using and displaying them with your hand-stitched embroideries. Together they'll be picture perfect!

~Kathy

redwork houses

FINISHED SIZE

Embroidery: 2½" × 4½"
Framed piece: 5" × 7"

Here's a chance to showcase embroidery in a new way, rather than stitching it into a pillow or tote bag. These petite scenes are adorable when matted with wool and the artwork at the back of the book and then framed. Make just one or make a set of three or four to fill a special niche in your home.

Materials

Materials are for one framed piece.

7" × 9" rectangle of cream print for embroidery background

3" × 5" rectangle of red wool

Red variegated pearl cotton, size 12 (Valdani P1), or embroidery floss for stitching

3" × 5" rectangle of lightweight fusible web

Permanent marker or pencil

FriXion pen or other removable fabric marker

Fray Check seam sealant

Pinking shears

Fabric glue

Decorative mat of your choice (pages 60–78)

Picture frame with 5" × 7" opening

Embroidery

1 Choose a design from the embroidery patterns on pages 12–13 (to match the photos) or from pages 20–21, 28–29, 36–37, or 46–47.

2 Center the cream print over the embroidery pattern. Be careful to align the sides of the rectangle outline with the threads of the fabric to keep the design on the straight grain. Trace the rectangle onto the cream print using a permanent marker or pencil. Use a removable fabric marker to trace the design inside the rectangle.

3 Referring to "Embroidery Stitches" on page 57 and using one strand of pearl cotton or two strands of floss, embroider the design, following the embroidery key for the chosen pattern.

NO KNOTS, PLEASE

Because the embroidery will be fused to the wool, try not to make knots on the back of the embroidery. Refer to "No-Knot Embroidery" on page 56.

4 When the embroidery is complete, press well from the wrong side.

5 Position the fusible web on the wrong side of the embroidery, aligning it with the drawn line on the right side. Use a window or light box to help with this. It doesn't have to be exact, just close. Fuse in place, following the manufacturer's directions.

6 Trim the embroidery to 2½" × 4½" (which is just inside the marked lines) and gently remove the paper backing from the fusible web.

7 Carefully apply a very small amount of Fray Check around the edges of the embroidery and allow it to dry.

Finishing

1 Center the embroidered piece on the red wool rectangle, then fuse it in place following the manufacturer's directions.

2 Use pinking shears to trim the wool, leaving ⅛" all around the edge of the embroidery.

3 Referring to "Decorative Mats for Framing" on pages 60–78, choose a mat design. You can either cut it out or make a color photocopy. If you would like to have a professional reproduce the art for you at a copy shop or office-supply store, permission is granted on the copyright page.

4 Trim the mat to 5" × 7", adjusting as needed so that it will fit in the frame.

5 On the back of the wool, place a small drop of fabric glue at each corner, then center the embroidered piece on the mat and apply pressure to adhere.

6 Place the embroidery in the frame and secure, using the backing that came with the frame.

Alternate Colorway

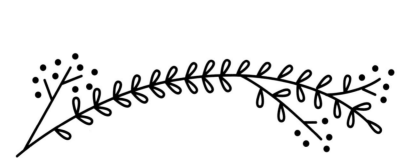

Embroidery Patterns

House and Heart

Embroidery Key

----- Backstitch

◯ Lazy daisy

- - - Running stitch

——— Stem stitch

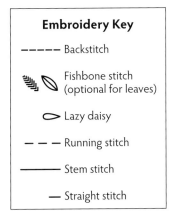

House and Garden

Straight stitch

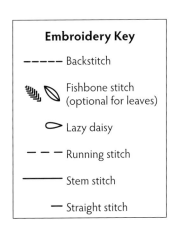

House on a Hill

Embroidery Key

- - - - - Backstitch

Fishbone stitch
(optional for leaves)

⟋ Lazy daisy

– – – Running stitch

—— Stem stitch

— Straight stitch

Embroidery Key

- - - - - Backstitch

Fishbone stitch
(optional for leaves)

⟋ Lazy daisy

– – – Running stitch

—— Stem stitch

— Straight stitch

bluework birds

FINISHED SIZE

Embroidery: 2½" × 4½"
Framed piece: 5" × 7"

Stitch a beautiful bluebird atop a blueberry branch or birdhouse, or take a peek into her nest. These bird designs are lovely in blue. Mat them on blue wool and use the artwork at the back of the book to continue the blue theme. Insert the stitched work into purchased frames to add sweet charm to any wall space in your home.

Materials

Materials are for one framed piece.

7" × 9" rectangle of cream print for embroidery background

3" × 5" rectangle of blue wool

Blue variegated pearl cotton, size 12 (Valdani P7), or embroidery floss for stitching

3" × 5" rectangle of lightweight fusible web

Permanent marker or pencil

FriXion pen or other removable fabric marker

Fray Check seam sealant

Pinking shears

Fabric glue

Decorative mat of your choice (pages 60–78)

Picture frame with 5" × 7" opening

Embroidery

1 Choose a design from the embroidery patterns on pages 20–21 (to match the photos) or from pages 12–13, 28–29, 36–37, or 46–47.

2 Center the cream print over the embroidery pattern. Be careful to align the vertical sides of the rectangle outline with the threads of the fabric to keep the design on the straight grain. Trace the rectangle onto the cream print using a permanent marker or pencil. Use a removable fabric marker to trace the design inside the rectangle.

3 Referring to "Embroidery Stitches" on page 57 and using one strand of pearl cotton or two strands of floss, embroider the design, following the embroidery key for the chosen pattern. Try not to make knots on the back of the embroidery, because it will be fused to the wool. Refer to "No-Knot Embroidery" on page 56.

4 When the embroidery is complete, press well from the wrong side.

5 Position the fusible web on the wrong side of the embroidery, aligning it with the drawn line on the right side. Use a window or light box to help with this. It doesn't have to be exact, just close. Fuse in place, following the manufacturer's directions.

6 Trim the embroidery to 2½" × 4½" (which is just inside the marked lines) and gently remove the paper backing from the fusible web.

7 Carefully apply a very small amount of Fray Check around the edges of the embroidery and allow it to dry.

Finishing

1 Center the embroidered piece on the wool rectangle, then fuse it in place following the manufacturer's directions.

2 Use pinking shears to trim the wool, leaving ⅛" all around the edge of the embroidery.

3 Referring to "Decorative Mats for Framing" on pages 60–78, choose a mat design. You can either cut it out or make a color photocopy. If you would like to have a professional at a copy shop or office-supply store reproduce the art for you, permission is granted on the copyright page.

4 Trim the mat to 5" × 7", adjusting as needed so that it will fit in the frame.

5 On the back of the wool, place a small drop of fabric glue at each corner, then center the embroidered piece on the mat and apply pressure to adhere.

6 Place the embroidery in the frame and secure, using the backing that came with the frame.

Alternate Colorway

Straight
stitch

Birdhouse

Embroidery Key

  Fishbone stitch
(optional for leaves)

█ Satin stitch

—— Stem stitch

— Straight stitch

Straight stitch

Nest

Straight stitch

Straight stitch

Bird on Branch

Embroidery Key

 Fishbone stitch (optional for leaves)

 Satin stitch

——— Stem stitch

— Straight stitch

Embroidery Key

Fishbone stitch (optional for leaves)

Satin stitch

——— Stem stitch

— Straight stitch

pretty
pillows

FINISHED SIZE

Embroidery: 6" × 16"
Pillow: 20" × 10"

Cozy up your bed or add comfort to a chair with these charming pillows. You can never have too many. Personalize them by choosing the five embroidery designs you love the most. Cheerful rickrack edging makes for a happy ending. Why not make one for yourself and one for a friend?

Materials

Materials are for one pillow.

8" × 20" rectangle of cream print for embroidery background

½ yard of dark print or stripe for pillow border and back

12" × 22" rectangle of batting

Dark red pearl cotton, size 12 (Valdani O547), or embroidery floss for stitching

2 yards of ½"-wide rickrack

FriXion pen or other removable fabric marker

Fiberfill for stuffing

Refer to "Embroidery Floss" on page 55 for the color used in the project shown on page 22.

Cutting

From the dark print or stripe, cut:
2 strips, 2½" × 42"; crosscut into:
    2 strips, 2½" × 16½"
    2 strips, 2½" × 10½"
2 pieces, 10½" × 11"

Embroidery

1   Choose five designs for the pillow front from the embroidery patterns on pages 12–13, 20–21, 28–29, 36–37, or 46–47.

2   Use a removable fabric marker to draw a 4¹³⁄₁₆" × 14⅜" rectangle onto the center of the cream print, then trace the rectangle outlines from the patterns inside the larger rectangle, aligning them side by side. Trace the embroidery designs inside the rectangles.

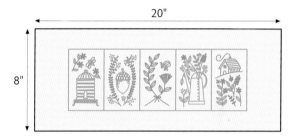

3   Use a removable fabric marker to draw a line ⅛" from each side of the shared vertical lines. Also draw a line ⅛" inside the entire outline. Measure and make a dot every ¼" on the drawn lines as shown. These will be guides for the fly stitch outlining.

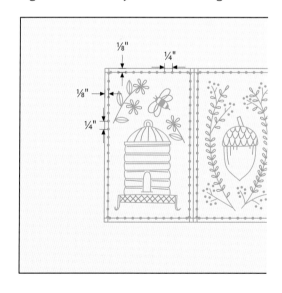

Assembling the Pillow Front

Use a ¼" seam allowance unless otherwise stated and press the seam allowances as shown by the arrows.

1. Sew the dark 2½" × 16½" border strips to the top and bottom of the embroidered piece. Sew the dark 2½" × 10½" border strips to the sides. The pillow front should measure 10½" × 20½", including seam allowances.

Make 1 pillow front,
10½" × 20½".

4. Referring to "Embroidery Stitches" on page 57 and using one strand of pearl cotton or two strands of embroidery floss, stitch the interior designs, following the embroidery keys for the chosen patterns.

5. Embroider the fly stitch using the ¼" dots and the drawn lines as a guide.

2. Place the pillow front on top of the batting. Pin or baste the layers together.

3. Quilt as desired. The pillows shown in the photos are machine quilted in the ditch of the dark borders.

4. Machine stitch the rickrack to the edges of the pillow front, beginning at the center bottom and leaving a 2" tail. The stitches should run through the center of the rickrack and be ¼" from the raw edge of the border. Miter the rickrack at the corners by turning it 90°.

5. When you reach your starting point, overlap the ends of the rickrack and angle them away from the pillow so that they will be

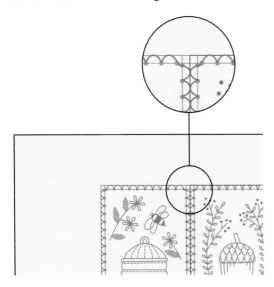

6. When the embroidery is complete, press well from the wrong side. Trim the piece to measure 6½" × 16½", keeping the design area centered.

in the seam allowance when the pillow front is sewn to the back.

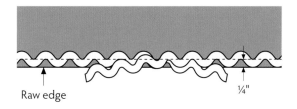

Raw edge   ¼"

Finishing the Pillow

1. Using a ¾" seam allowance (not ¼"), sew the two dark 10½" × 11" pieces together along the 10½" sides, switching to a basting stitch for about 5" in the middle of the seam and backstitching at the beginning and end of the basted section to secure. The pieced pillow back should measure 10½" × 20½", including seam allowances. Press the seam allowances to one side.

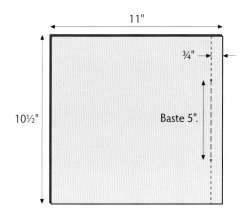

11"

¾"

10½"   Baste 5".

2. With right sides together and the pillow front on top, pin the pillow front to the back. Sew around all four sides, stitching on top of the rickrack stitches.

3. Clip the corners and excess rickrack.

4. Remove the basting stitches from the pillow back and turn the pillow right side out through the opening.

5. Stuff the pillow with the fiberfill and hand stitch the opening closed.

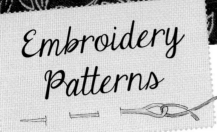

Embroidery Patterns

Straight stitch

Birdbath

Embroidery Key

  Fishbone stitch (optional for leaves)

Lazy daisy

Running stitch

Stem stitch

Straight stitch

Acorn

Bee Wreath

Elongated
fly stitch

Embroidery Key

- - - - - Backstitch

∨ Fly stitch

• French knot

◠ Lazy daisy

—— Stem stitch

Embroidery Key

- - - - - Backstitch

Fishbone stitch
(optional for leaves)

∨ Fly stitch*

◠ Lazy daisy

■ Satin stitch

—— Stem stitch

— Straight stitch

*Note that flower petals are
elongated fly stitches.*

garden decor

FINISHED SIZE

Embroidery: 2½" × 4½"
Framed piece: 5" × 7"

If you're a gardener, or even if you're not, here's an opportunity to stitch an indoor version of a cottage garden. A happy bird, a flitting bee, and cheerful flowers arranged in a watering can are matted on wool, combined with artwork from the back of the book, and framed to add summer cheer to your home all year.

Materials

Materials are for one framed piece.

7" × 9" rectangle of cream print for embroidery background

3" × 5" rectangle of black wool

Black, olive, and red pearl cotton, size 12 (Valdani O531, P2, and P1), or embroidery floss for stitching

3" × 5" rectangle of lightweight fusible web

Permanent marker or pencil

FriXion pen or other removable fabric marker

Fray Check seam sealant

Pinking shears

Fabric glue

Decorative mat of your choice (pages 60–78)

Picture frame with 5" × 7" opening

Embroidery

1 Choose a design from the embroidery patterns on pages 36–37 (to match the photos) or from pages 12–13, 20–21, 28–29, or 46–47.

2 Center the cream print over the embroidery pattern. Be careful to align the sides of the rectangle outline with the threads of the fabric to keep the design on the straight grain. Trace the rectangle onto the cream print using a permanent marker or pencil. Use a removable fabric marker to trace the design inside the rectangle.

3 Referring to "Embroidery Stitches" on page 57 and using one strand of pearl cotton or two strands of floss, embroider the design, following the embroidery key for the chosen pattern. Try not to make knots on the back of the embroidery, because it will be fused to the wool. Refer to "No-Knot Embroidery" on page 56.

4 When the embroidery is complete, press well from the wrong side.

5 Position the fusible web on the wrong side of the embroidery, aligning it with the drawn line on the right side. Use a window or light box to help with this. It doesn't have to be exact, just close. Fuse in place, following the manufacturer's directions.

6 Trim the embroidery to 2½" × 4½" (just inside the marked lines) and gently remove the paper backing from the fusible web.

7 Carefully apply a very small amount of Fray Check around the edges of the embroidery and allow it to dry.

Finishing

1 Center the embroidered piece on the wool rectangle, then fuse it in place following the manufacturer's directions.

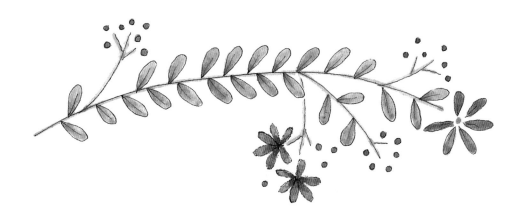

2 Use pinking shears to trim the wool, leaving ⅛" all around the edge of the embroidery.

3 Referring to "Decorative Mats for Framing" on pages 60–78, choose a mat design. You can either cut it out or make a color photocopy. If you would like to have a professional at a copy shop or office-supply store reproduce the art for you, permission is granted on the copyright page.

4 Trim the mat to 5" × 7", adjusting as needed so that it will fit in the frame.

5 On the back of the wool, place a small drop of fabric glue at each corner, then center the embroidered piece on the mat and apply pressure to adhere.

6 Place the embroidery in the frame and secure, using the backing that came with the frame.

Embroidery Patterns

Fence

Embroidery Key

Fishbone stitch
(optional for leaves)

• French knot

▀ Satin stitch

——— Stem stitch

— Straight stitch

Watering Can

Beehive

Embroidery Key

 Fishbone stitch (optional for leaves)

• French knot

◯ Lazy daisy

— Stem stitch

Embroidery Key

----- Backstitch

✕ Cross-stitch

 Fishbone stitch (optional for leaves)

◯ Lazy daisy

- - - Running stitch

■ Satin stitch

— Stem stitch

— Straight stitch

bowl fillers
and sachets

FINISHED SIZE
Embroidery: 2½" × 4½"
Bowl filler or sachet: 4" × 6"

These sweet bowl fillers or sachets make wonderful gifts for anyone who enjoys and appreciates unique, handcrafted items. Of course, you can make them for yourself too! Make a sachet for each of your closets or stitch several to fill a decorative basket or favorite bowl.

Materials

Materials are for one bowl filler or sachet.

7" × 9" rectangle of cream print for embroidery background

8" × 12" rectangle of dark print for border and backing

5" × 7" rectangle of batting

Permanent marker or pencil

FriXion pen or other removable fabric marker

Red or blue variegated pearl cotton, size 12 (Valdani P1 or P7), or embroidery floss for stitching

DMC 6-strand embroidery floss for cording*

Cord maker*

*See "Resources" on page 79. One skein of floss will yield enough cording for two bowl fillers or one sachet. As an alternative to making cording, you can use ⅔ yard of chenille yarn or other trim for the bowl filler. For the sachet, you'll need 1⅓ yards of trim.

Additional Material for Bowl Filler

Fiberfill for stuffing

Additional Materials for Sachet

Dried lavender flowers for stuffing

10" length of ⅜"-wide ribbon for hanger

2 cream buttons, ⅝" diameter

Cutting

From the dark print, cut:
2 strips, 1" × 5½"
2 strips, 1" × 4½"
2 rectangles, 3½" × 4½"

Embroidery and Quilting

1. Choose a design from the embroidery patterns on pages 12–13, 20–21, 28–29, 36–37, or 46–47.

2. Centering the embroidery pattern, trace it onto the cream fabric rectangle with a permanent marker or pencil. Do not trace the rectangle outline.

3. Referring to "Embroidery Stitches" on page 57 and using one strand of pearl cotton or two strands of floss, embroider the designs, following the embroidery key for the chosen pattern. When the embroidery is complete, press well from the wrong side.

4. Use a removable fabric marker to draw a 3½" × 5½" rectangle around the stitching, keeping the design centered.

5. Center the embroidery, right side up, on the batting. Quilt as desired, keeping the stitches inside the drawn rectangle. The bowl fillers on pages 38–39 are hand quilted using diagonal crosshatch lines spaced ½" apart. The sachet on page 44 is hand quilted with echo quilting around the designs.

6 Because quilting may have slightly altered the size of the drawn rectangle, measure the quilted and embroidered piece and trim to 3½" × 5½".

Assembling the Bowl Filler or Sachet

Use a ¼" seam allowance and press the seam allowances as shown by the arrows.

1 Sew the print 1" × 5½" border strips to opposite sides of the embroidered piece. Sew the print 1" × 4½" border strips to the top and bottom. The pieced front should measure 4½" × 6½", including seam allowances.

Make 1,
4½" × 6½".

2 Place the two print 3½" × 4½" rectangles right sides together and align the raw edges. Stitch along the 4½" side, switching to a basting stitch for about 2" in the middle of the seam and backstitching at the beginning and end of the basted section to secure. The pieced back should measure 4½" × 6½".

Baste 2".

3 With right sides together, pin the front to the back and sew all the way around.

4 Clip the corners, remove the basting stitches from the back, and turn right side out.

5 With the embroidered side up, stitch in the ditch of the border seams, through all layers, to create a flange.

6 If you're making the bowl filler, insert fiberfill through the opening in the back. If you're making a sachet, fill with lavender.

7 Hand stitch the opening closed.

Adding the Cording

The cording in the samples was created using a cord winder and six strands of DMC floss.

1 To make the cording, cut a 110" length of the DMC floss. Referring to "Cord Making" on page 58, make a 22" length of cording using all six strands of floss. If you're making the sachet, cut a second length of floss, 120" long, to make a 24" length of cording to go around the outside of the sachet.

2 Pin the center of the 22" length of cording to the center top of the embroidery. Align the cording with the border seam, across the top and down one side of the project, until you reach the center of the bottom edge. This is where you will begin stitching the cording.

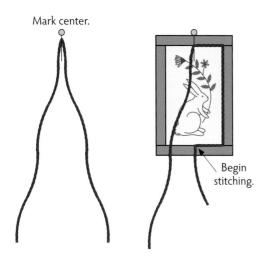

Mark center.

Begin stitching.

3 Whipstitch the cording to the front along the border seam all the way around, using one strand of the same floss used for the cording.

4 Tie a knot where the cording ends meet at the center of the bottom. Also tie knots 1" past the center knot on each cord and trim the excess. The bowl filler is complete. Continue with the instructions that follow to finish the sachet.

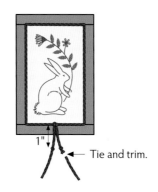

1"

Tie and trim.

Finishing the Sachet

1 Leaving a 2" tail at the beginning, start whipstitching the 24" length of cording to the outer edge of the sachet, ½" from one of the top corners. Continue until you reach the starting point. Where the two ends of the cording meet, tie a small tight knot and trim the ends to ½".

½" ← Tie and trim.

2 Trim the ribbon as desired—keep it long to go over a doorknob or shorten it to go over a hanger. Sew the ribbon to the top corners of the sachet with the buttons so that the ends of the cording are hidden.

Embroidery Patterns

Teacup

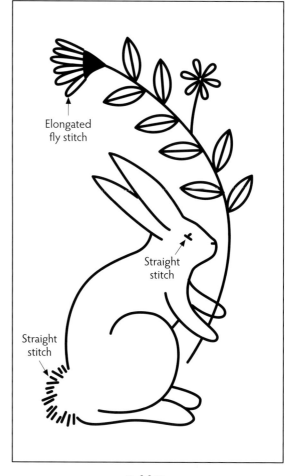

Elongated fly stitch

Straight stitch

Straight stitch

Rabbit

Embroidery Key

 Fishbone stitch (optional for leaves)

• French knot

Lazy daisy

—— Stem stitch

Embroidery Key

- - - - - Backstitch

 Fishbone stitch (optional for leaves)

∪ Fly stitch*

Lazy daisy

Satin stitch

—— Stem stitch

— Straight stitch

Note that uppermost flower petals are elongated fly stitches.

Potted Plant

Straight stitch

Cat

Bowl Fillers and Sachets

note cards

FINISHED SIZE

Embroidery: 3" × 5"
Folded card: 4½" × 6¼"

Share your stitching skills when sending these lovely note cards. There's a design suitable for most occasions, whether the sentiment is "happy birthday," "thank you," or simply "thinking of you." The card you tuck into the envelope will be unique, personal, and have a maker's special touch. What better way to let friends and family know how much they mean to you!

Materials

Materials are for one card.

5" × 7" rectangle of tan solid for embroidery
   background*
Cream embroidery floss (DMC #739) for stitching
2½" × 4½" rectangle of lightweight fusible web
FriXion pen or other removable fabric marker
Blank note card, size A6, and envelope**

Use a woven fabric that will ravel easily, such as weaver's cloth.

**Packs of note cards and envelopes can be found at most craft-supply stores. You can also make your own using cardstock. Cut the cardstock to 6¼" × 9". Fold it in half to form a card that measures 4½" × 6¼".*

Embroidery

1. Choose a design from the embroidery patterns on pages 12–13, 20–21, 28–29, 36–37, or 46–47.

2. Center the tan fabric over the embroidery pattern. Be careful to align the sides of the rectangle outline with the threads of the fabric to keep the design on the straight grain. Use a removable fabric marker to trace the design onto the fabric.

3. Referring to "Embroidery Stitches" on page 57 and using two strands of floss, embroider the designs, following the embroidery key with the chosen pattern. The embroidery will be fused to the note card, so try not to make knots on the wrong side when stitching. See "No-Knot Embroidery" on page 56.

4. When the embroidery is complete, press well from the wrong side.

Finishing

1. Use a removable fabric marker to draw a 2½" × 4½" rectangle around the stitching, keeping the design centered.

2. Position the fusible web on the back of the embroidery, aligning it with the drawn rectangle. Hold the fabric up to the light to see the rectangle. When it's aligned with the rectangle, fuse the web following the manufacturer's instructions.

3. Trim the background fabric to 3" x 5". Gently pull the fabric threads to create a fringe ¼" wide around all four sides.

¼"

4. Remove the paper backing and fuse the embroidered piece to the center of the card front using a dry iron. Iron carefully and slowly to prevent discoloration of the paper.

Embroidery Basics

In this section you'll find some of the basic information you'll need for hand embroidery. If you're new to sewing and quilting, you can find additional helpful information at ShopMartingale.com/HowtoQuilt, where you can download free illustrated how-to guides on everything from rotary cutting to binding a quilt.

Tracing the Design

When it comes to tracing or transferring the embroidery design onto fabric, I recommend using a light box. Start by pressing the waxy side of a piece of freezer paper to the wrong side of the fabric. The freezer paper will stabilize the fabric and make tracing easier. Tape the design in place on the light box, and then center the fabric on top of the design and secure it in place. I like to use a Pilot FriXion pen to trace lightly over the design. (The ink in a Pilot FriXion pen will disappear with the heat of an iron.) A fine-point washable marker, a ceramic pencil, or a mechanical or wooden pencil with a fine, hard lead will also work. When tracing onto a dark fabric, a white chalk pencil works well.

If you don't have a light box, you can tape the design to a window or use a glass-topped table with a lamp underneath.

Needles

There are many types of hand-sewing needles, each designed for a different technique. Needle packages are labeled by type and size. The larger the needle size, the smaller the needle (a size 1 needle will be longer and thicker than a size 12 needle). An embroidery needle is similar to a Sharp, but with an elongated eye designed to accommodate six-strand floss or pearl cotton. You may want to try a size 7, 8, or 9. I'm often asked what kind of needle I use for embroidery, and the answer is Kathy Schmitz size 7 embroidery needles, which are perfect for 12-weight pearl cotton or two strands of embroidery floss (KathySchmitz.com).

ABOUT THE FABRIC

One of my favorite background fabrics for embroidery is Moda Crackle. It has a subtle design that creates a lovely texture next to the embroidery stitches. I used this for the background of most of the projects in this book.

Hoops

Embroidery hoops are used to keep the fabric taut, but not tight, while stitching. Hoops are available in wood, metal, and plastic, with different mechanisms for keeping the fabric taut. Any type of hoop is fine, so take the time to find one you're comfortable with. I don't use a hoop, but if you'd like to use one I suggest trying a hoop that is 4", 5", or 6" in diameter to see what you prefer. Remember to always remove the fabric from the hoop when you've finished stitching for the day.

Embroidery Floss

All of the projects in this book except the note cards were stitched using a single strand of Valdani pearl cotton, size 12. Six-strand embroidery floss is also an option, and I used that for the note cards. Use two strands of floss or one strand of pearl cotton for all of the embroidery. Note that several of the pearl cottons that I used are variegated. The projects will have a different look if stitched in a solid-color pearl cotton or floss.

Quilt as Desired

It's easiest to quilt through as few layers as possible, so I don't put a backing fabric under the batting. I never use a hoop, but I do baste together the batting and embroidered piece well. If it's a small project, I just baste around the outside.

I have a hard time using a thimble, so I usually end up with sore fingers. Sometimes I'll use one of the stick-on "thimbles," and that works well for me. I think the most important thing is to enjoy the process and not get too caught up in the technical aspects.

Project	Generic Color	Valdani Color	Valdani #
Redwork Houses	Red variegated	Old Brick	P1
Bluework Birds	Blue variegated	Withered Blue	P7
Green Pillow	Dark green variegated	Dark Green	PT8
Red Pillow	Dark red	Burnt Chocolate	O547
Garden Decor	Almost black	Black Nut	O531
	Olive green	Olive Green	P2
	Red	Old Brick	P1
Bowl Fillers	Red variegated	Old Brick	P1
Sachet	Blue variegated	Withered Blue	P7
Alternate Colorways	Almost black	Black Nut	O531
	Olive green	Olive Green	P2
	Red variegated	Old Brick	P1

No-Knot Embroidery

I like to use the "waste knot" technique to keep the back of embroidery work free of knots and loose threads that might show through.

1   Cut the thread 2" to 3" longer than the usual 18" length to allow extra thread for the waste knot. Thread the needle and knot the thread.

2   Insert the needle into the background from the right side, at least 2" from where you'll begin stitching. (Increase this distance to 3" until you gain practice with this method.) Bring the needle up where you want to begin; the knot will be on the right side of the work.

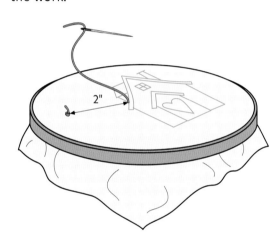

3   Stitch until you are near the end of the thread. With the thread on the wrong side, weave the thread end under previous stitches to secure it. Trim the excess thread.

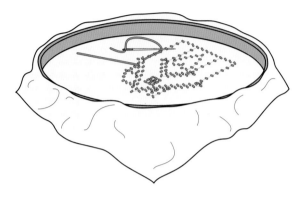

4   Go back and cut off the knot on top of the work. Thread the end on the needle and weave the end through the stitches on the back.

Embroidery Stitches

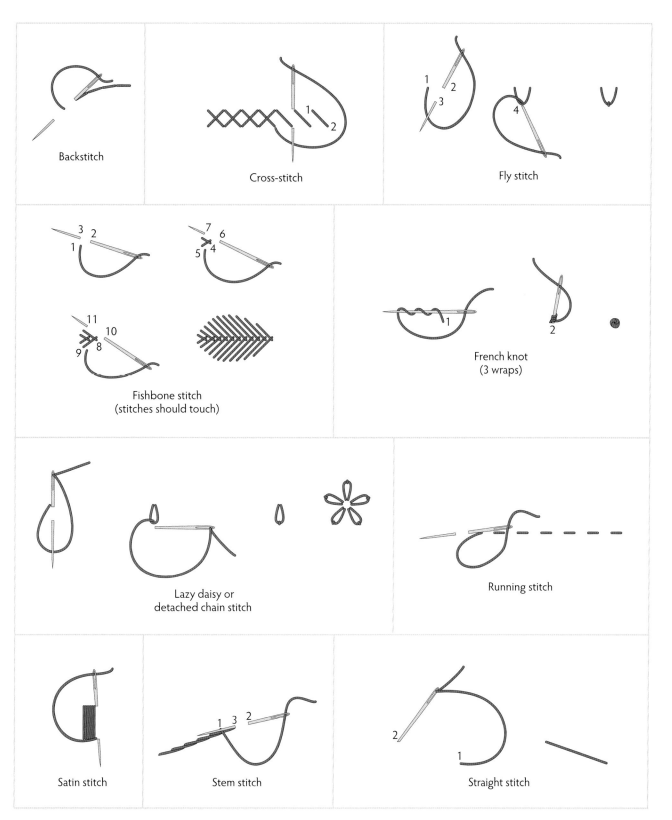

Backstitch

Cross-stitch

Fly stitch

Fishbone stitch
(stitches should touch)

French knot
(3 wraps)

Lazy daisy or
detached chain stitch

Running stitch

Satin stitch

Stem stitch

Straight stitch

Cord Making

Adding a simple handmade twisted cord to cover seams or to add a color accent can turn a sweet little project into a classic treasure. Some of the projects in this book are finished using cording made from six strands of floss and a cord maker. A cord maker is relatively easy to use and lots of fun.

1 Cut a length of floss following the project instructions. (Each project lists the length of floss needed to make the cording. The ratio of floss to finished cording is about 5:1.)

2 Tie the ends together to form a large loop. Place the knot end on the hook of the cord maker (fig. 1).

3 Attach the loop end of the floss to a hook or other stationary object and start winding. It's very important to keep the tension taut while winding. Just keep going! Remember, you must keep constant tension on the floss (fig. 2).

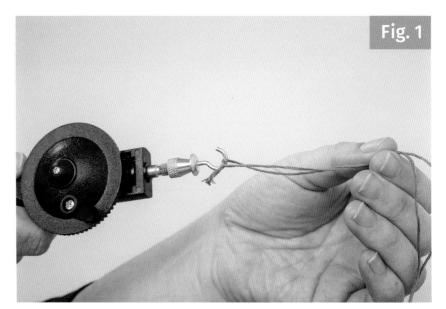

Fig. 1

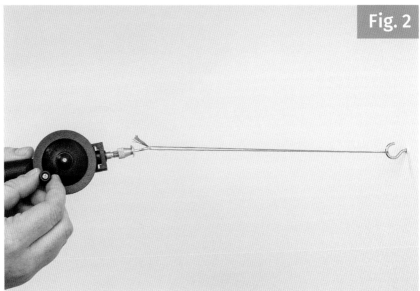

Fig. 2

CORDING TIP

I make cording so often that I decided to screw a teacup hook into the side of my bookcase.

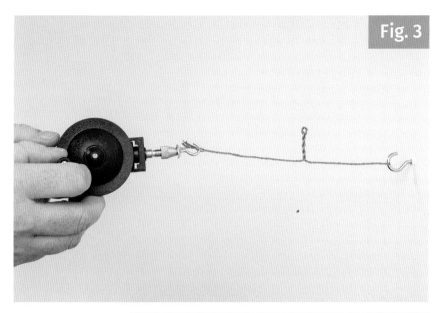

Fig. 3

4 Do the "kink test" by keeping the cording taut and slowly bringing it closer to the hook on the cord maker. If the cording kinks and twists together, it's ready (fig. 3).

5 Keeping the tension taut, remove the end of the cording from the cord maker. Place the hook of the cord maker over the cording at about the center of its length. Keeping a grip on the cord maker, bring the two ends of the cording together with your other hand. Remove the other end from the teacup hook. Hold both ends in one hand, with the ends pinched together, and hold the cord maker in the other hand (fig. 4).

Fig. 4

6 Let go of the cord maker and let it spin and spin! When it stops spinning in one direction, remove it from the cording before it starts spinning in the opposite direction. Tie a knot at the ends you're holding.

Decorative Mats for Framing

Throughout this book, photos show framed embroideries matted with decorative backgrounds, such as the cherry branches mat shown above. The original watercolor backgrounds are reproduced on pages 62–78, and you can cut them out or photocopy them to use when framing your embroideries, covering the quotations in the middle with your embroidery. To create a coordinating group of framed pieces, consider cutting out or photocopying the decorative mats and framing them as is, with the quotation in the center.

This page is intentionally left blank for photocopying other side.

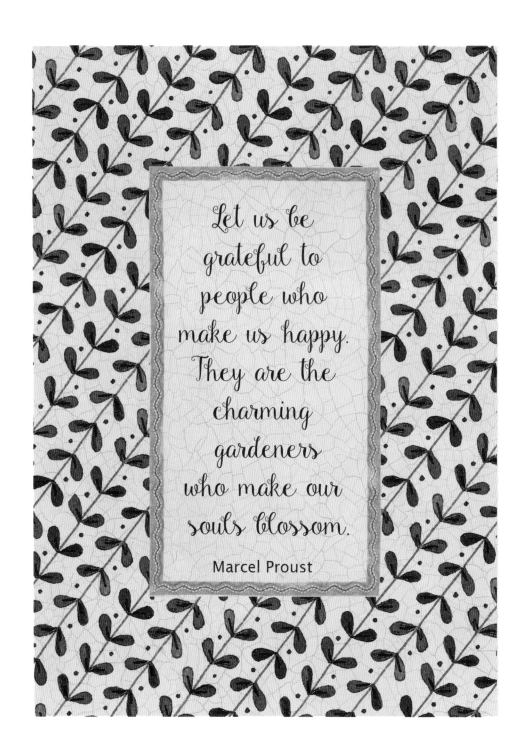

*Let us be
grateful to
people who
make us happy.
They are the
charming
gardeners
who make our
souls blossom.*

Marcel Proust

Permission is granted to photocopy this page for personal use only.
Trim the photocopy to fit a 5" × 7" frame opening.

✳

Adopt the pace of nature: her secret is patience.

Ralph Waldo Emerson

Permission is granted to photocopy this page for personal use only.
Trim the photocopy to fit a 5" × 7" frame opening.

This page is intentionally left blank for photocopying other side.

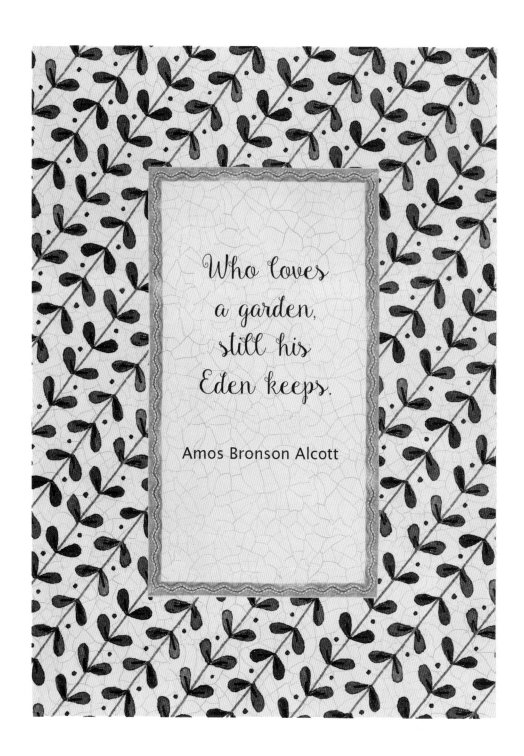

Who loves
a garden,
still his
Eden keeps.

Amos Bronson Alcott

Permission is granted to photocopy this page for personal use only.
Trim the photocopy to fit a 5" × 7" frame opening.

This page is intentionally left blank for photocopying other side.

above all, i must have flowers, always and always.

Claude Monet

Permission is granted to photocopy this page for personal use only.
Trim the photocopy to fit a 5" × 7" frame opening.

This page is intentionally left blank for photocopying other side.

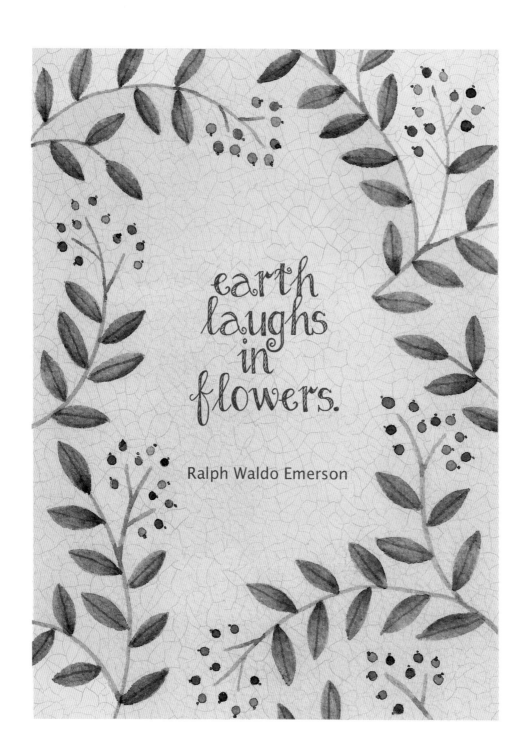

earth
laughs
in
flowers.

Ralph Waldo Emerson

This page is intentionally left blank for photocopying other side.

blossom
by blossom
the spring
begins.

Algernon Charles
Swinburne

Permission is granted to photocopy this page for personal use only.
Trim the photocopy to fit a 5" × 7" frame opening.

This page is intentionally left blank for photocopying other side.

I value
my garden
more for
being full
of blackbirds
than cherries,
and very
frankly give
them fruit
for their
songs.

Joseph Addison

Permission is granted to photocopy this page for personal use only.
Trim the photocopy to fit a 5" × 7" frame opening.

This page is intentionally left blank for photocopying other side.

Friendship
is a
sheltering
tree.

Samuel Taylor Coleridge

Permission is granted to photocopy this page for personal use only.
Trim the photocopy to fit a 5" × 7" frame opening.

This page is intentionally left blank for photocopying other side.

One
touch of
nature
makes
the whole
world
kin.

William Shakespeare

Permission is granted to photocopy this page for personal use only.
Trim the photocopy to fit a 5" × 7" frame opening.

Embroidery Pattern Index

Acorn	29	House and Garden	13
Bee Wreath	29	House and Heart	12
Beehive	37	House on a Hill	13
Bird on Branch	21	Nest	21
Birdbath	28	Potted Plant	47
Birdhouse	20	Rabbit	46
Cat	47	Teacup	46
Fence	36	Watering Can	37

Resources

Cord Maker
KathySchmitz.com

Valdani Pearl Cotton
RustyCrow.com

Embroidery Needles
KathySchmitz.com

About the Author

When Kathy Schmitz was growing up, her mom always made sure that she and her sisters had an abundance of creative craft supplies at their fingertips. The girls were encouraged to draw and sew to their hearts' content, and many of their masterpieces were taped to the walls of their mom's sewing room. Kathy knew from a young age that this was what she wanted to do for a living! After many trials and errors, and jobs at banks and the like, Kathy says she is lucky enough to be what she always dreamed of being as a little girl—a designer. Kathy has designed fabric for Moda since 2002 and has had her own pattern company since 2007. Put a needle and thread or pen and ink in her hand, and she's a happy camper!

Kathy lives in beautiful Portland, Oregon, with her sweet hubby, Steve. Although her sons are grown and on their own, they are always close to her heart.